Profit or Principles

Investing Without Compromise

Dwight Short

D1115745

Profit or Principles:
Investing Without Compromise

Published by Austin Brothers Publishing
Keller, Texas
www.austinbrotherspublishing.com

ISBN 978-0-9853263-7-1

This and other books published by Austin Brothers Publishing can be purchased at www.austinbrotherspublishing.com

Cover Design: Jay Cookingham

Printed in the United States of America

2012 -- First Edition

Contents

Foreword

I am always inspired by spiritual high achievers.

One example in the Bible is a man named Caleb. He was given a promise: "Surely the land on which your foot has trodden shall be an inheritance for you and your children forever, because you have wholly followed the LORD my God" (Joshua 14:9, ESV). As we read the rest of Caleb's story, we see that he attempted and accomplished much for God.

Why was Caleb such a high achiever? Joshua 14:9 tells us. He wholly followed the Lord. Caleb's life forces me to ask myself a tough question: "Am I wholly following the Lord or have I settled for partially following Him?"

The man who wrote this book is one of those spiritual high achievers. Dwight Short seeks to wholly follow the Lord. Yes, he's a humble man who admits that he fails. But his heart's desire is to follow the Lord fully as a good steward of his time, talent, and treasure. Dwight is seeking to hear a "Well done!" from the lips of our Lord.

When it comes to managing the treasure entrusted to him, Dwight is passionate about seeking to steward, not just his sharing and his spending, but even his savings, wisely. For Dwight, investing is an important part of what it means for us to follow the Lord wholly, not just partially.

Money is not just a neutral medium of exchange. It's actually a powerful spiritual force in our lives, a force that can be positive or negative. How we handle our treasure will either draw us toward God or lead us away from Him. Our investments are opportunities for spiritual decline or spiritual development in our lives. Spiritually, our money has both upside potential and downside risk.

Several years ago, Dwight asked my wife, Mary-anne, and me to attend a National Association of Christian Financial Planners conference as his guests. We had a great time of rest. More importantly, we learned about Biblically Responsible Investing – a concept that helps believers follow the Lord wholly.

Even though our investment funds were handled through our denomination, we learned through a screening process that some of our funds were indirectly supporting causes that violated our convictions. So, with Dwight's help, we found a financial advisor that helped us reinvest our resources in an even more biblically responsible way. Now, we have a greater peace of mind that our treasure is invested in things that God approves.

Early in his career, before Dwight became a financial advisor and consultant, he was a teacher and a coach. Maryanne and I are grateful that Dwight is still teaching and coaching. He has equipped us with a new tool, Biblically Responsible Investing, so we could live more consistently with our convictions.

In *Profits or Principles: Investing without Compromise*, you will be encouraged, inspired, and challenged as you go with Dwight on a journey. He will take you into a story with Todd and Elise as they grow in their understanding about Biblically Responsible Investing. Dwight will help you gain insights from scripture like Matthew 25 and Romans 13-14. He will show you how to make some changes to help you wholly follow the Lord with your investments.

Dwight writes, "Christian investors ought to differ in the way they conduct themselves—because God really is the owner of all they have." I know first-hand that Dwight isn't just a teacher, coach, and advisor who knows the way and shows the way. He's a player-coach who also goes the way.

Remember: Spiritual high achievers are those who wholly follow the Lord. *Profits or Principles* is an important tool in stewardship training to help many of us see a blind spot in our discipleship portfolio. Dwight is on a mission to serve us so that our investments are more and more pleasing to Christ.

Rick Duncan
Founding Pastor, Cuyahoga Valley Church

Introduction

In this book you will be introduced to Todd and Elise. They could be your neighbors. They could be part of your small group from church or they might just sit next to you on Sunday mornings. They might remind you of your brother or sister or another family member. As you get to know them, you will learn about their walk with the Lord and indirectly yours as well. Their story begins as they discover God wants to teach them about the ramifications of their investments, but there will be other lessons that will come to light as well.

When we are alert to God's calling in our lives, the real world is a challenging place to live out our faith. If we could stay in church all day every day, it might be easier, but in fact we must relate to happenings in our world where a lot of messy things happen. Todd and Elise encounter this thru what seemed like an innocent investment and then must decide what to do when confronted with uncomfortable truths. The difficulty for readers is that the reality of their situation comes to life so clearly that you will want to follow their strategies to see what you might consider in your own lives.

Almost one out of every five shares of stock being traded on the market today is held in portfolios that screen for issues of ethics, values, or sinfulness. There are more investors and advisors who are working to help identify the correct stocks and bonds for their holdings to reflect their values than ever before. Investors are more convinced than ever that their performance will not only not suffer from doing this, but in fact believe they may actually do better. For Christians the calling that they are not just investing for themselves but in fact are investing God's funds make this even more compelling.

You may have some of the same concerns that Todd and Elise have about making changes, but in both their case and yours, it is more important to learn about your options and most of all about what God is calling you to do. In a world dominated by materialism, secularism, and technological obsession it is a challenge to figure out how individuals can make a difference and have an impact when their investments represent such a small part of the total. Despite all the odds of fighting against the "principalities" of this world, God still works thru our lives and situations to teach us things when we least expect it.

You too will find areas of your life that you never considered before when you walk along with Todd and Elise. Open your heart and mind for the journey by reading Romans 13 and 14 before moving forward. This was Ron Blue's suggestion to me before writing my first book, Kingdom Gains. Welcome to the journey and welcome to the chance to serve God in a new way!

A New Story

There's something comforting about the familiar sound of the front tires turning into your own driveway late at night. It's difficult to imagine the gravel at your house sounds differently against rubber tires than gravel from somewhere else so the feeling is probably nothing more than the sense of belonging, of being in the place where we are most comfortable. Whatever it is, that is the feeling that greeted Todd as he steered his luxury sedan up the sloped driveway and pulled to a stop in the garage. By Todd's own standards it was a late evening. He was normally relaxing in bed or, more likely, deep in sleep by this time of the night.

Although Todd's wife Elise was sitting in the passenger's seat, neither of them had spoken more than a sentence on the drive home. It was not that they were angry with one another; they were both too tired to think of anything to say. It had been a very long day, one of the longest either could remember. In spite of the length it had been a good day, very good indeed.

Todd and Elise's daughter Sarah, their only child, was married earlier in the afternoon. The wedding was a magnificent affair, just the right amount of glamour to make it worthy of a feature in a bridal magazine but far short of being considered opulent. It was the culmination of more than a year's worth of planning. Sarah wed her longtime sweetheart and Todd was glad, or was it relieved, the day was drawing to a conclusion. He had no reservations about Sarah and her new husband. In fact, if Todd had the opportunity to choose a husband for his amazing daughter, Christopher would have been his first choice.

As they climbed upstairs to their bedroom, Todd and Elise held hands. They enjoyed the moment, the feeling of accomplishment. The two of them together had built something special – a nice home, full bank account, successful business, a wonderful daughter, and now time to reflect.

Todd was the first to speak as they entered the bedroom. "You know, things are going to change now," he said.

Elise was fully aware that her life was already experiencing changes since Sarah was gone, but she wasn't sure what Todd meant. "What are you saying?"

"We've spent our entire life to this point preparing for what's going to happen in the next part of life," Todd replied. "We have to change our focus."

She wasn't sure what that meant but Elise was too tired to give it much thought. The emotions of the wedding and the busyness of the reception had taken her energy. She was confident that her thinking could wait for a good night's rest.

Todd's energy was equally spent and it didn't take long before they were both deep in sleep, resting in the comfort that comes from accomplishing a significant goal.

■ ■ ■ ■ ■

Diligence was one of Todd's best qualities, one that did not allow him to stay in bed even on Sunday morning. He was up with the sun. His normal routine was to brew a cup of coffee and when the weather allowed, perch in his favorite chair on their backyard deck. He tried to start every morning with his coffee and Bible. Today was no exception.

If you had to choose one word to describe Todd's life at this very moment, the word contentment would be a good choice. Everything that most people would look to for happiness was at his fingertips. He and Elise had worked hard to provide for Sarah and to set her on the way to success. College was expensive, the wedding as well, but it was worth it to see her beaming as the center of attention. But now it was time to think about the next phase of life.

By most definitions, Todd was a successful businessman. Like many who succeed in business, he began as a teenager, washing cars and changing oil. The tenacity instilled by his parents turned him into an entrepreneur waiting to happen. It was obvious Todd was going to be successful; the only question for the teenager was what field he would choose.

Like many, he turned his passion into his business. His first job was with an old man known only as Wilson. It was a used car lot, essentially six thousand square feet of cracked asphalt with a two-room wooden office building standing alone in the center of the lot. The structure was covered with eye-catching bright blue paint that was known all over town as "that blue box on sixth street." Streamers with those various colored triangle, flag-shaped flaps were stretched from all four corners of the building to metal posts located on all four corners of the lot. They had flapped and faded in the sun for so long that it was not easy to tell the red ones from the yellow ones.

Wilson always had between twenty and thirty cars parked under the banners, waiting for just the right customer. This was not one of those tote-the-note kind of used car lots where they make their money on financing and will send a big guy with a smashed nose to collect if you miss a payment. Wilson sold clean, good quality cars. In fact, he did a little financing, but his preference was for the customer to deal with his own bank.

Wilson was probably seventy years old when he

hired Todd to shine cars and keep the lot looking clean. He came to work every day wearing a white shirt and a dark tie. The only time he ever loosened the collar was at night when he removed the tie to get ready for bed. His reputation was as well known around the city as was his blue office building. Wilson was considered a rare creature in the used car business—a man of integrity.

In fact, Todd heard Wilson's philosophy of business so often that it eventually became a credo for his own life. A day did not pass without Todd hearing Wilson say, "always tell the truth" and "always do the right thing." Any problem he ever brought to Wilson, those words were the only answer he ever received. That is precisely how he ran the business. Customers had no reason to worry they were being sold a used car with problems. Wilson would tell them everything he knew about the car—good or bad. If a customer ever returned with a complaint, he could be confident Wilson would do everything he could to make it right. Some would say it was not a profitable business plan but it worked, allowing Wilson to feed his family his entire life.

Polishing and cleaning cars became more than Todd's way of earning spending money. It became his passion. Once he accumulated a small stash of money, he purchased a well used sedan, fixed all the problems, shined it up, and sold it for a significant profit. It was such a good experience he did it again. And again. And again. Todd knew how to fix cars and sell cars, a winning combination. It took twenty years, but he took the small used car lot that he opened at age twenty and parlayed it into the largest dealership in the city.

It had been a long time since he had approached an engine with a wrench but Todd was just as good at managing people as he was tools.

$$\blacksquare \ \square \ \blacksquare \ \square \ \blacksquare$$

Todd always considered himself a Christian although he was not serious about his relationship with Christ until after he and Elise were married. Church attendance was important to her and she insisted they go together, every Sunday, as a couple. It didn't take long until Todd began to listen to the sermons more carefully. However, the real turning factor was the relationships they developed with friends, those who were committed to giving their lives in service to the church. Over the years, four couples became very close to one another. They were strong pillars in the church and well-known Christian leaders in the community.

Reading his Bible every morning was important to Todd. Just because of the big day yesterday, he was not deterred from beginning this Sunday with a word from God's Word. His current reading cycle had him in the Gospel of Matthew. The Gospels were always favorites for Todd–he loved reading stories about Jesus. Coming to the middle of the twenty-fifth chapter, he read through the familiar story of the Parable of the Talents. This story about the wealthy master who entrusted his money with his slaves made him feel good about himself. Giving a tithe to the church, supporting community charities, and generously responding to special appeals was a way of life for Todd.

Closing his Bible, Todd stood up just as Elise came out on the deck, cup of coffee in hand. He was glad to see her. She was especially important to him now. For the first time in more than two decades, they were on their own. They could plan their lives according to their desires, not the needs of their daughter or anyone else.

Elise gave Todd a hug and then both sat down at the table, Elise with her fresh cup of coffee and Todd with one that was nearly empty. "What did you mean last night when you said it's time to change our focus?"

"I just meant that we have accomplished our main goals with Sarah—she has a college degree and is beginning her own family with a great young man. We've done well, but now it is time to move on," continued Todd.

For the next ten or twelve minutes Todd and Elise continued their discussion about the next step and how they should focus their lives. Certainly they did not finish the conversation but it was time to get ready and go to church.

◼ ◻ ◼ ◻ ◼

Sunday morning church was a highlight in Todd's week. He loved the music, appreciated the pastor's sermon, and most of all he looked forward to being with friends who shared his values. He was not real outspoken at church but since he had been there for so many years, everyone knew who he was and what he did.

He knew the congregation well and Todd suspected that he and Elise were probably some of the wealthiest people in the church. They certainly felt a responsibility to do their part financially—and they did. They were committed to giving at least a tithe of their income and were always generous whenever a special offering was presented. In fact, during their last building program, Todd wrote out a check for one hundred thousand dollars. That is one of the reasons he appreciated Jesus' story of the Master and the talents. It was always an affirmation of what he already believed and practiced.

Since they were dragging from the busy wedding day, Todd and Elise were a few minutes late on this particular Sunday morning. Rather than sitting in their normal spot toward the front, they slipped into one of the pews in the back of the sanctuary. They knew folks would understand, in fact, nobody really expected them to be there any way.

As anticipated, the music was good—the choir sounded exceptional today. Todd was feeling a little nostalgic about being in this sanctuary. He could still picture the flowers, pink and white ribbons, and flickering candles that filled the room just a few hours earlier. There had not been time to study the video yet, but Todd knew he and Sarah were an impressive sight as they marched down the center aisle, arm in arm. He is not embarrassed to admit several tears slowly trickled down his cheek before arriving at the altar. But, when the pastor stood in the pulpit to preach this day, Todd put his reflections aside, grabbed his Bible, and prepared himself to follow along.

To his surprise, the pastor began by announcing his sermon text was from the Gospel of Matthew, chapter twenty-five. Talk about a coincidence. "The pastor must be on the same reading schedule," Todd thought to himself. "Maybe God is trying to tell me something!"

As usual, the pastor carefully expounded the scripture passage, bringing it to life with memorable stories and appropriate applications. But he didn't say anything that struck Todd as new or different from what he already believed. He didn't feel especially inspired to do anything or to change his thinking about anything. Perhaps it was nothing more than a coincidence. Probably it was God's way of affirming what Todd already knew and lived.

Todd and Elise tried to keep a low profile as they were leaving the church service. They had seen all their friends the day before at the wedding and they were both still a little exhausted. They were hoping for a quick exit. It was not to be.

Just as they stepped out the door into the sunshine, Todd heard the words, "Hey, Mr. Watson!"

He never liked being referred to as "Mr. Watson." That was his father's name, but he knew it was simply a polite manner of speech.

When Todd turned to his left to answer the voice, he noticed a young man with closely cropped brown hair dressed in khaki pants and a pale-colored golf shirt. He had seen him occasionally at church but didn't know his name. The man appeared to be nervous, almost as if he forced himself to look Todd in the eye. Todd assumed the man had something to say about the wedding, perhaps a quick word of congratulations. Todd returned the eye contact and said, "Can I help you?"

"Yes sir," he replied, "I want to speak with you for just a short minute." With that he realized he had not properly introduced himself. "I'm Robert Wells," he inserted quickly. "We've never really met although I see you often at church. My wife and I've been attending for about six months now."

"Good to meet you Robert. What I can I do to help?" Todd tried not to sound impatient but he and Elise really wanted to get away as quickly as possible. As he spoke, Todd continued taking short strides in the direction the parking lot, hoping the intruder would not stop him for long.

Sensing that Todd was not interested in a long conversation, Robert quickly got to the point. "I work with a group of people who are trying to help families and new mothers. We work hard to speak out against abortion and we provide counseling and assistance to young women who are pregnant."

Todd was aware that his church was often on the frontlines when it came to the issue of abortion so he assumed Robert was a part of that ministry.

"I have a question for you," Robert spoke almost apologetically.

"Sure, what is it?"

"Do you own the building at fifth and Washington, on the northeast side?" he asked.

"Fifth and Washington just north of downtown? I don't think so. My dealership is out on Hastings on the west side of town," replied Todd.

"The building I'm talking about is owned by Lawson Investments. I was told you were part owner of that company."

"Lawson, yah, that's a company run by some of my old college buddies from way back. They asked me to be a part of their group, but I don't have anything to do with running the company. They buy old buildings, refurbish them and rent them out. That makes sense. That's an older part of town," It was obvious Todd was searching his memory. "I think I technically own twenty percent of the company but other than cashing a check every once in a while I don't pay much attention to what they are doing. Why do you ask?"

"There's a medical clinic at Fifth and Washington

that leases space from Lawson Investments. They're the primary abortion providers in the city. We've been trying for years to shut them down but nothing has worked. Then I discovered Lawson Investments and your ownership and I got to thinking you might be able to help us," suggested Robert.

Todd was caught off guard for a moment. He really had no idea about the investments his friends made. In fact, he never gave it any thought. They were all good guys, several of them active in church.

"I don't know," he spoke slowly trying to give himself some time to think. By now he had stopped his slow pace toward the parking lot. "Perhaps I can talk with them and see what's up. Let me think about this and get back with you."

"That would be great," said Robert with a hint of hope in his voice.

The men shared phone numbers before they shook hands. Todd noticed that Elise was growing a little impatient waiting for him. She was not close enough to hear the conversation so she had no idea what he was doing.

"What was that all about?" she asked as Todd walked toward her.

"That guy has given us something to think about," he replied quickly as they made their way to the parking lot.

On the drive home, Todd explained the situation to Elise. He knew she would be worked up about it because she was very outspoken in her opposition to abortion. For several years Elise worked as a volunteer counselor at the church's pregnancy helps center, encouraging young women to choose birth rather than abortion.

He was right. As soon as they entered the house, she wanted Todd to call his friends and do something about the situation. Todd understood her passion but was able to assure her that it would be best to wait and visit with them personally during the coming week.

■ ■ ■ ■ ■

Since Todd and Elise had a quiet day of rest planned once they arrived home from church, he had a lot of time to think. In light of their conversation about a new direction from this moment on, he wanted to spend time reflecting on what that meant. It was also curious to him that God kept reminding him about the Parable of the Talents, both in his morning reading and the pastor's sermon. Maybe there was more to being a good steward than he thought.

Early Monday morning, Todd made a phone call to his college friend Brett. It was Brett who got him involved with Lawson Investments. In fact, the business took Brett's last name even though his financial investment was only marginally larger than the one made by Todd. After a few minutes of catching up on news, Todd and Brett made arrangements to have lunch together on Tuesday.

Todd had shown very little interest in the business so he was careful not to sound accusatory. "Brett, I was told that we own a building that is being leased to a medical clinic in the downtown area."

"That's right," said Brett, "It's the old Sullivan building on Washington Street. It was remodeled and has been a real money maker for us, staying at close to ninety-percent occupancy. It is one of our best performing properties. Why do you ask?"

"This fella came up to me at church and said the medical clinic is the biggest abortion provider in the city. Do you know anything about that?"

"I don't guess I've ever paid attention. They've been real good about paying their rent on time so I haven't given any thought to what they are doing," answered Brett. "Are we supposed to?"

"I think we should," said Todd.

Brett wasn't sure how to respond. After a short silence he said, "Let me talk to the other investors and see what they think we should do. I would hate to lose such a good tenant; they pay a lot of rent and have never been a problem."

Before they finished the conversation and the meal, Todd and Brett agreed to talk on the phone by the end of the week and touch base about the situation.

During the week, Todd spent a great deal of time and mental energy reflecting on what he should do about the clinic and his investment. He realized it probably had something to do with the Parable of the Talents. He couldn't get Jesus' story out of his mind.

Elise suggested they simply sell their interest in the business and then they would be free from the responsibility for what the investment firm did with their money. But, Todd was not convinced that was the proper approach. After all, since he was a part owner, he did have some say in how the business operated. Selling off their ownership would not bring about any change. He was beginning to think that good stewardship meant more than just making a profit. As the week progressed, Todd became more and more convinced he needed to take responsibility and do everything within his power to change this situation.

When Brett called late in the week, the news was not all good. Some of the other investors didn't feel like it was a problem and thought they should be more concerned with the money and holding on to a good tenant.

"Are they open to discussing the situation?" Todd asked.

"You know all of them, Todd," Brett answered. The other three investors were old college friends. "They're willing to sit down and discuss the situation if you really think it is that important."

Todd still wasn't sure about the proper approach. All he knew was that he had a decision to make. Either get out of the partnership or do everything he could to change the partnership. He and Elise spent a great deal of time discussing what they should do and praying for wisdom. They finally concluded that the best thing they could do was talk with the other partners. It was not enough just to wash their hands of the situation as long as they still had some influence.

After speaking with Brett once again, they decided to arrange a partner's meeting, primarily to discuss what should be done about renting space to the medical clinic. Todd was not a dynamic speaker but he was a salesman, he knew how to make his case. As he waited for the meeting, he continued to pray.

One afternoon Elise asked a question that took his thinking in another direction. She said, "Do we own any other companies?"

"No, just the car dealership," Todd answered quickly.

However, the question kept coming back to him. It finally dawned on him that they do own shares in other companies, many other companies. They have money invested in the stock market so technically they are company owners.

"You know Elise, when I told you we don't own any other companies that's not entirely correct."

"What do you mean?" she replied.

"We have money in the stock market and we own shares in several mutual funds. In a sense we own parts of a lot of different companies," he answered.

"Do we know anything about those companies,"

Elise innocently asked. "What if some of them provide abortions or other stuff that is wrong?"

Somewhat perplexed Todd said, "I don't have any idea. I don't even know how we would find out. I have folks who take care of that stuff for us, I don't even know if they know."

Todd realized he had more to do than prepare for a meeting with his investing partners. It was time to give serious consideration to all of his financial investments. Jesus' Parable of the Talents was beginning to take on a life of its own in his thinking. The one driving issue that kept coming to the forefront of his thinking was the fact that God had given him money to invest and handle. Because of that, it was important to use it in the best way possible. He really wanted to be one of the servants who were considered faithful.

An Old Story

Running the risk of stating the obvious I will declare that Jesus was a master storyteller. He used stories for every occasion–to explain a theological truth, to correct a common misunderstanding, to respond to a legitimate question, to provide insight into an eternal principle, and to explain His own ministry. His stories were impactful and memorable. He always took common experiences and ordinary people and wove them together in a beautiful manner that illustrated a great truth. One such story is often referred to as the Parable of the Talents.

> *"Again, it will be like a man going on a journey, who called his servants and entrusted his wealth to them. To one he gave five bags of gold, to another two bags, and to another one bag, each according to his ability. Then he went on his*

journey. The man who had received five bags of gold went at once and put his money to work and gained five bags more. So also, the one with two bags of gold gained two more. But the man who had received one bag went off, dug a hole in the ground and hid his master's money.

"After a long time the master of those servants returned and settled accounts with them. The man who had received five bags of gold brought the other five. 'Master,' he said, 'you entrusted me with five bags of gold. See, I have gained five more.'

"His master replied, 'Well done, good and faithful servant! You have been faithful with a few things; I will put you in charge of many things. Come and share your master's happiness!'

"The man with two bags of gold also came. 'Master,' he said, 'you entrusted me with two bags of gold; see, I have gained two more.'

"His master replied, 'Well done, good and faithful servant! You have been faithful with a few things; I will put you in charge of many things. Come and share your master's happiness!'

"Then the man who had received one bag of gold came. 'Master,' he said, 'I knew that you are a hard man, harvesting where you have not sown and gathering where you have not scattered seed. So I was afraid and went out and hid your gold in the ground. See, here is what belongs to you.'

"His master replied, 'You wicked, lazy servant! So you knew that I harvest where I have not sown and gather where I have not scattered seed? Well then, you should have put my money on deposit with the bankers, so that when I returned I would have received it back with interest.

"'So take the bag of gold from him and give it to the one who has ten bags. For whoever has will be given more, and they will have an abundance. Whoever does not have, even what they have will be taken from them. And throw that worthless servant outside, into the darkness, where there will be weeping and gnashing of teeth.'" (Matthew 25:14-30).

This particular story is about a man who went on a journey. He was not an ordinary man, a neighbor from down the street. Obviously he was a man who had servants because the story describes three of them in significant detail. It appears that he was also a man of great wealth. He is the kind of man who did not want the word to get out that he was leaving town and his house was sitting empty. He wanted to make sure his wealth was properly taken care of by his servants.

Jesus typically told stories that His listeners could easily identify with, finding themselves among the characters. However, on this occasion He spoke of a man that his audience could only dream about. This man leaving on a journey was nothing like anyone in the crowds that gathered around Jesus.

The context of this parable is a discussion between Jesus and His disciples. It was the final days of His earthly ministry and He was aware they would be facing some difficult times ahead with many questions about the future. He used the opportunity to speak to them about some of the events they could anticipate. His intention was to inform and encourage them to stay strong and faithful.

Pressed between a discussions about his return, which they had no possibility of understanding at that point in history, and a discussion about God's criteria for judgment, Jesus told the story of the talents. It was information that was probably not too valuable at that particular time but would become more so in the next few weeks. Obviously, this story is about God's coming judgment and the standard He will use in making that judgment–an important concept for all of us.

Like the father in the story of the Prodigal Son, this traveling man provides an image of God and how He acts. The owner of the gold will be returning and this is what will happen when he does. None of us may be able to relate to the wealthy traveler, but every one of us can see ourselves in the servants. If you will be honest, you will find yourself in this story.

In first century Palestine, wealth was identified by owning land, animals, clothing, and precious metals. In the Sermon on the Mount, Jesus had earlier warned about storing up earthly treasures because they are susceptible to moth, rust, and thieves. In this story, the Parable of the Talents, Jesus describes the man's wealth as being precious metal, most likely gold. We know that because he speaks of the weight of the man's stuff.

The reason this story has become known as the Parable of the Talents is because the word "talent" was used by Jesus. He was not speaking of some innate ability to sing, paint, dance, or some other capability you might find in a talent show. A "talent" was a term for measuring weight, like we would use "ounce" or "pound."

To fully understand Jesus' story, it is important to grasp the enormity of the amount of gold this man left in the charge of his servants. One talent was equivalent to three thousand shekels, which, in our terminology is nearly seventy-six pounds. This man left eight talents with his servants. In other words, he left them with the responsibility of taking care of more than six hundred pounds of gold.

To make the point even more clear, let's calculate the value of this much gold according to the price of gold today. It sells for more than sixteen-hundred dollars per ounce, which means he left nearly sixteen million dollars worth of gold in the hands of these three servants. He certainly had a great deal of trust in their ability. You and I read the word "talent" and don't think much about it. However, Jesus followers would have immediately understood that Jesus was speaking about an impressive amount of money, far beyond their experience.

An interesting feature of the story is that each servant received responsibility according to their ability. The money was not randomly distributed nor was it evenly disbursed. He knew his servants and he was aware of their ability to handle money. The master anticipated success expecting them to live up to their capability. It seems that might be the very definition of responsibility–the ability to respond.

By giving them responsibility, the master was providing them an opportunity–an opportunity to prove themselves and to reveal their relationship with him. The obvious implication of Jesus' story is that God gives to each of us according to our ability. He knows us and what we can handle. In fact, later in the story it becomes obvious the master knew his servants well. The one who was given the least was the one who failed the most. If we can comprehend this truth it will free us from always striving to get more stuff. Our receiving is according to our ability. The way to increase our receiving is to increase our ability. In other words, if we want to be trusted with more then we must be more faithful with what we already have.

The way to attain riches is not to win the lottery or gain some other kind of windfall. It is the result of diligent work and putting our resources to work in order to demonstrate our ability. That is the reason this book was written and probably the reason you are reading.

One servant had the ability to handle ten million

dollars, another ability to handle four million, and the third had the ability for two million. Each was set up to succeed. The master gave them everything they needed to fulfill their ability. "But remember the Lord your God, for it is he who gives you the ability to produce wealth, and so confirms his covenant, which he swore to your ancestors, as it is today" (Deuteronomy 8:18).

In first century Palestine, there was not a stock exchange or a plethora of investment vehicles. There were not a lot of options if you had to do something with a large amount of money. They did have banks. In fact, upon his return the master asked why his money was not deposited in the bank for interest. However, they were certainly not FDIC insured and would have been a risky investment.

Typically, when a person wanted to make money with money, he would be involved in some type of commerce. It could have been purchasing fine clothing or material, or perhaps dealing in precious metals and jewels. For a more long term perspective the money could be used to purchase land. In order to turn a profit required a very hands-on approach to dealing with the money.

For most people, the safest thing to do with a treasure was to bury it in the ground. Another story Jesus told concerned a man who stumbled across a buried treasure so he went to purchase the field in order to claim the treasure (see Matthew 13:44). It seems this treasure had been buried a long time, so long the owner forgot about it. In the Parable of the Talents, the third servant took this course of action, burying the master's money in order to keep it safe. It was probably the safest route but as he discovered, there was no return on the money.

The first two servants immediately put the money to work. We are not told what they did, how they invested, but they were successful. Essentially they doubled the money. We are not told how long the master was gone but apparently it was a significant amount of time. For two investors to realize a hundred percent return meant they both either hit a big windfall or they took advantage of time.

If you have invested very much money you are probably aware of the "Rule of 72." It provides a simple way to determine the length of time it will take to double an investment once you know the rate of return. If you divide the number "72" by the rate of return it will tell you the length of time needed. For example, 10% interest divided into "72" reveals it takes 7.2 years to double the investment. If the rate of return is 3% then the length of time is nearly 24 years.

The servants were each given a large amount of money, a significant amount of time, and a responsibility to increase the investment. Money plus time should be a valuable combination.

The wording Jesus used to describe the activity of the first two servants is identical. They reported the money had been doubled, the master praised them for the faithfulness, and expressed they would be receiving even greater responsibility. Finally, they were invited to share in the master's happiness.

However, the third servant had a different report. 'Master,' he said, 'I knew that you are a hard man, harvesting where you have not sown and gathering where you have not scattered seed. So I was afraid and went out and hid your gold in the ground. See, here is what belongs to you.' Reacting out of fear, this servant hid the master's gold in the ground. Remember, that was probably the safest place for money in first century Palestine. The rationale he gave was his understanding of the master as being a harsh businessman.

The difference between this servant and the first two is clear. They understood the master wanted them to put the money to work. He was afraid of the master, so much so that he chose the safest course of action, which was inaction.

The response of the master was swift and sure. He condemned the servant for his misunderstanding and fear, took away the gold that had been left to his charge, and give it to the servant who already had ten talents, one who was obviously more suited for the responsibility. One of the more fascinating statements in the parable is that the man should have at least put the money in the bank to earn a small interest. Obviously, doing nothing with the master's money was not an option.

It seems safe to conclude that God wants us to

be profitable with His money. It is not good steward-ship to simply hang on tight to what He gives to us, He expects it to be managed and turned into something of increasing value. Also, everything we know about God suggests He is more interested in why and how we do something than He is the result. For example, the Pharisees were meticulous keepers of the Sab-bath yet Jesus continually criticized them for their hard hearts and oppressive rules. He did not criticize them for keeping the Sabbath but for the way they kept the Sabbath.

The same is true with their tithing. They were strict tithers, calculating down to the very last penny, but listen to what He said to them:

> *"Woe to you, teachers of the law and Phari-sees, you hypocrites! You give a tenth of your spices--mint, dill and cummin. But you have neglected the more important matters of the law--justice, mercy and faithfulness. You should have practiced the latter, without neglecting the former.* (Matthew 23:23)

Essentially, Jesus said it is good to tithe but it is more important why and how you tithe. Therefore, it only makes sense that God is not simply interested in how much money we make from our investments but how we did it.

Myriads of folks have become rich by investing

their money in pornography, alcohol, gambling, and other things we can be confident are not pleasing to God. Hugh Hefner has made a sizable fortune printing filth. The owners of Budweiser have accumulated a good return on their money by encouraging drunkenness. Donald Trump can credit much of his wealth to casinos in Atlantic City and Law Vegas. In spite of the success of these investors it is impossible to imagine that God is unconcerned with how they made their money.

It is hard to imagine God being pleased when anyone makes a profit at the expense of other people. That is exactly what happens when we invest in certain types of companies. For example, an investment in a company that profits from gambling depends on people losing money at casinos, online websites, race tracks, and other venues.

It all starts with your orientation and your understanding of what the Bible says about you and "your" possessions. This flows directly into stock or mutual fund ownership as well. Whose name is on the certificate or the brokerage account that is holding these investments? It may be you, you and your spouse jointly, or a trust. Maybe it is your company or one of its benefit plans that has the earthly title listed as "owner." It may even be your retirement plan or the church's endowment fund that is listed as the owner. But who really owns it?

The most difficult concept for us to reconcile as

Christians is who really owns the assets that are titled in our earthly names. Once you realize and believe that God owns it and you are merely the short-term steward of all the assets listed it will give you a new appreciation for what this book is all about. This principle alone is why Christian investors ought to differ in the way they conduct themselves—because God really is the owner of all they have.

When Jesus first told the story in Matthew 25, it was clear to every listener that all the gold (talents) belonged to the master. The slaves were merely entrusted to handle the master's money. At no time did the money belong to them. That is a simple illustration of all of life. None of us own anything. Even the most successful business person must acknowledge that everything belongs to God and all we are doing is handling God's money on His behalf.

There are many lessons to be learned from Jesus' story, but for our purposes we will focus on just two. First, we will be held accountable for what is entrusted to us. The servant who was given five talents was expected to answer for the way he used five talents. The servant with two had to answer for his use of two. The servant with just one talent did not have to answer for more than the one placed at his disposal. In other words, we cannot excuse ourselves by complaining that we had very little to manage. All of us have a responsibility before God.

The second lesson is that we will be judged on the

basis of the profitability of our investments. The two servants who doubled their money were praised and the one servant who simply chose not to lose anything was condemned. However, as we have noted, financial return is not the only concern of the master. Judgment will also focus on what we did with the master's money. Was it used beneficially as well as profitably? Did the investment not only increase the bottom line but did it also provide value to other people? These are the kinds of questions the Master will ask when we are called to give account of our stewardship.

It is also important to remember the context of Jesus' story. He was telling it to remind us that judgment is inevitable. We will be held accountable for our stewardship of the possessions God places in our hands. All of us want to hear, "Well done, good and faithful servant!"

Writing Your Story

As we have seen from the fictional story of Todd and Elise and the parable of Jesus concerning the master leaving money with his servants, we have a responsibility with the way we handle God's money. As you no doubt already know, God owns everything. The Psalmist said, "The earth is the Lord's and everything in it." The prophet Habakkuk added, "'All the silver and all the gold is mine,' says the Lord." This is the most basic principle of biblical stewardship. We all live as the servants in Jesus' story. Everything we have really belongs to the master and we are simply managing it until he returns.

This is an easy truth to give our mental assent to but it is not so easy in practice. The reason we struggle is because the world keeps giving us a conflicting message. We constantly receive subtle reminders that the stuff belongs to us—our name on the bank account, the car title, the investment account, etc. It makes us wonder if the servants in Jesus' parable felt the same way. The master left for a long time. I wonder if they were tempted to think he is not returning or he had forgotten.

It's hard to accept the concept that God owns it all because we want to think of ourselves as being in control of our lives and our assets. This tendency for self-reliance and rebellion against anything that makes us accountable is counter to our human instincts for independence. The sooner we can recognize God's sovereignty, the easier it will be to exercise our role in acting with a "limited power of attorney" (limited by our lifetime) to represent God's interests as we seek His will. This includes all areas of financial management. Once we become shareholders, there is no other option than to be Biblically Responsible Investors.

A frequent attitude among Christians is that we are only expected to steward ten percent of our income, or what people call the tithe. This causes many to feel free to do what they want with money after they give their tithe to the church. Even more startling is that only ten percent of our net worth is in actual cash so even if we do tithe, technically we are only giving God ten percent of ten percent. Remember, it all belongs to Him.

The very nature of servanthood means the servant owns nothing. The listeners of Jesus' parable would have clearly understood this truth. A servant is not able to choose to only give a portion to the master;

it all belongs to the master.

Since the money in your investment account belongs to God it is most appropriate to handle that money in a way that is pleasing to Him. He is not simply interested in how much profit we make with His money, He is equally concerned with the way that profit is earned. It is lazy and irresponsible to simply give the money to someone else and let them do what they want as long as it earns a little profit. When the master returns, it will not be enough to say, "I put the money in some good funds and let others take care of it!"

God has entrusted the money into our hands and it is up to us to make good decisions about how the money is used. This does not mean that we must sell all our stocks and bonds and give the money to mission organizations or charity of some kind. As we learned from Jesus' parable, there is certainly nothing wrong with using money to make more money. However, it does mean we must do more than simply give a tithe of our monthly income to the Lord and use the rest according to our own discretion.

How does an investor use investments as a good steward? How is it possible to know if my investments are doing good and not harm? There is a way for you to be comfortable with how your money is being utilized that does not require you to sacrifice the ability to be profitable.

What is Biblically Responsible Investing

An awareness of how money is invested is not a new concept. As far back as the 18th century, more than one hundred years prior to the Civil War, the Religious Society of Friends (we generally refer to them as Quakers) practiced a very simple form of responsible investing. The wealthier farmers among them owned a few slaves and a few Quaker merchants invested in slavery, but for the most part, Quakers were more focused on the moral concerns surrounding the legitimacy of slavery. In 1688, the Germantown New Jersey Quaker meeting sent a letter to the New Jersey Yearly Meeting warning Friends against the evils of slavery. By the eighteenth century many colonial Quakers were speaking out against profiting from slavery. It soon became uncomfortable in colonial Quaker communities for white Friends to be served by black Friends who were not "savages" but Christians, who spoke the same language, wore the same clothes, ate the same food, worked the same work as their masters, and followed the same religion.

One by one, family by family, meeting by meeting, eighteenth century American Quakers stopped participating in slavery. They chose to divest themselves from the slave trade, purely on ethical and moral reasons which had nothing to do with financial profit and loss. They choose to avoid any financial involvement with companies that profited from the slave trade.

Subsequently in the mid-1700s, John Wesley, Founder of Methodism, was a very outspoken advocate for believers practicing good stewardship. He had a great deal to say about money, which he considered the second most important subject in New Testament teaching. The Methodists, along with the Quakers are generally credited with bringing this understanding of money and investments to the New World.

Consequently, many credit them with being among the first proponents of what we call today Socially Responsible Investing (SRI). The movement was fueled by Christians early in the twentieth century who wanted to avoid what they called "Sin Stocks." These were companies that promoted smoking, drinking, and gambling. This type of investing was fueled by Prohibition in the 1920s and was even utilized after the development of mutual funds.

The modern movement received its greatest impetus in the 1960s as a result of the Vietnam War, civil rights, and equality for women. In the 1970s, concerns expanded to include labor-management issues and nuclear weapons. The movement grew exponentially in the 1980s due in large part to success in making an impact on the issue of apartheid in South Africa. Environmental disasters like Chernobyl and the Exxon Valdez were also significant factors.

As you might conclude from this list of issues, Socially Responsible Investing was essentially the domain of social liberals, including Christians from the more liberal wing of the church. These investors typically avoided investments in the alcohol, gaming, tobacco, nuclear power, and weapons/defense industries. Conversely, they were attracted to companies that supported such issues as worker's rights, women's rights, environmental protection, gay/lesbian rights, fair lending practices, and low income housing.

Modern day Evangelical Christians are not strong proponents of some of the issues supported by most Socially Responsible Investors and there are other issues that matter to them. Consequently, they have created an approach that is more in line with their beliefs. The term used for this approach is Biblically Responsible Investing (BRI).

Before I explain the difference between Socially Responsible Investing (SRI) and Biblically Responsible Investing (BRI) it is necessary to understand the nuts and bolts of how it works. First, we must understand what it means to screen an investment. Screening typically involves building an investment portfolio through a process that explicitly eliminates or deliberately includes certain stocks or bonds based on the activities of those companies. The performance can be assessed across a range of factors or it is possible to focus on only one issue. Screened mutual funds or annuities are an important and common example of this strategy. In other words, companies are evaluated on their performance based on specific criteria. For example, an investor chooses to avoid companies that support alcohol sales and consumption. They would obviously screen out breweries and other manufacturers of alcohol, but it might also include companies that own restaurants and retail outlets that sell alcohol. This means that mutual funds would also be evaluated based on the companies that are a part of that fund.

Socially Responsible Investors created a standard list of screens that included issues important to them, but as we noted earlier, did not cover all the issues that concerned many evangelical Christians. Therefore, Biblically Responsible Investing was created to better reflect the concerns of Christian investors. The typical screens used in BRI are the following:

- **Tobacco Manufacturers and vendors of tobacco**

    Don't you know that you yourselves are God's temple and that God's Spirit lives in you? If anyone destroys God's temple, God will destroy him; for God's temple is sacred, and you are that temple (1 Corinthians 3:16-17).

There is no doubt that tobacco, whether it is smoking or other ways of using, is physically harmful. It not only damages and kills the bodies of those who smoke but it also harms others through second-hand smoke. Despite this, smoking in the United States is down only slightly, despite all of the legal efforts to ban smoking in many places. Meanwhile, the tobacco companies have taken their advertising to countries overseas and in developing parts of the world where consumption in many places is at all time highs. It seems like such a no-brainer that anyone would waste money on such disgustingly filthy products—but it's happening, and Christians are contributing to the problem.

- **Abortion**

> *Jesus said, "Let the little children come to me, and do not hinder them; for the kingdom of heaven belongs to such as these"* (Matthew 19:14).

> *"See that you do not look down on one of these little ones. For I tell you that their angels in heaven always see the face of my Father in heaven"* (Matthew 18:10-11).

> *"The God who made the world and everything in it is the Lord of heaven and earth and does not live in temples made by hands. And he is not served by human hands, as if he needed anything, because he himself gives all men life and breath and everything else"* (Acts 17:24-25).

Life is a gift from God, and companies that work in the abortion industry are considered unacceptable investments by many Christians. These include: manufacturers of abortion materials, hospitals that perform abortions for profit when not required by state laws, insurance companies that pay for abortions as a benefit, contributors to Planned Parenthood and other agencies supporting abortion, and researchers who harvest stem cells from aborted children.

Without debating if there is ever an abortion that God would approve, I can contend with great certainty that God is pro-life! It is quite apparent to me that our Lord must be in great agony when observing how prevalent this procedure is in our world today. In the United States alone, it is estimated that we have killed 50 million babies since the decision in Roe v. Wade. Some point to the fact that the annual number of abortions has dropped to about a million babies as a positive trend. But that is not enough. Just thinking about the waste of human talent that we are missing brings tears to the eyes of many people. If any other childhood disease was killing a million infants every year, there would be a major movement to eradicate that disease and that issue would be the centerpiece of every political campaign. The least Christians can do is to check the companies in their portfolios to make sure they are not funding Planned Parenthood or research that is making body parts a centerpiece of the profit margin for their earnings.

- **Pornography** – This include producers of "adult" film and music, distributors of smut, Internet providers and content providers emphasizing porn, adult entertainment companies, and credit card companies specializing in porn.

> *Do not love the world or anything in the world. If anyone loves the world, the love of the Father is not in him. For everything in the world— the cravings of sinful man, the lust of the eyes and the boasting of what he has and does—comes not from the Father but from the world* (1 John 2:15-16).

> *Who may ascend the hill of the Lord? Who may stand in his holy place? He who has clean hands and a pure heart, who does not lift up his soul to an idol, or swear by what is false* (Psalm 24:3-4).

The ease of access of this type of material on the Internet has made this one of the most pervasive problems for all segments of our society. The Christian church is not immune from this problem as studies have shown this to be as common in the homes of believers as well as non-believers.

- **Entertainment** - Anti-family producers and advertisers

> *You used to walk in these ways, in the life you once lived. But now you must rid yourselves of all such things as these: anger, rage, malice, slan-*

der, and filthy language from your lips (Colossians 3:7-8).

> *Therefore, I urge you, brothers, in view of God's mercy, to offer your bodies as living sacrifices, holy and pleasing to God—this is your spiritual act of worship. Do not conform any longer to the pattern of this world, but be transformed by the renewing of your mind. Then you will be able to test and approve what God's will is—his good, pleasing and perfect will* (Romans 12: 1-2).

The range of media products, including music, movies, television, radio, and Internet games, is often just the tip of the iceberg when it comes to how pervasive smut has become in our society. Because someone has to produce the garbage and someone else has to propagate it, there are many places for investors to be on the watch for violations. It is important to be concerned with not only those who produce filthy material but also those who sponsor it through advertising.

- **Lifestyles** - Financial support for the expansion of lesbian, gay, bi-sexual and trans-gender lifestyles, also known under the acronym LGBT or sometimes GLBT, companies that provide employee training that purports the normalcy of the LGBT agenda, active involvement of corporate funds in the advancement of the LGBT agenda.

The look on their faces testifies against them; they parade their sin like Sodom; they do not hide it. Woe to them! They have brought disaster upon themselves. Tell the righteous it will be well with them, for they will enjoy the fruit of their deeds (Isaiah 3:9-10).

These alternative lifestyles have grown to the rank of great importance in the corporate world as these groups seek to establish their credibility in the same way racial and gender differences received attention and action. For example, there are court cases pending which seek to eliminate gender-defined public restrooms because they discriminate against those with sexual variances to the biblical norm of uniquely male and female. Companies find themselves in a great deal of turmoil in interpreting various employment discrimination laws in light of many court tests on these issues.

Organizations that refuse to be intimidated by the ACLU and other left-wing protagonists on same-sex benefits are to be applauded and perhaps included in one's portfolio.

•   **Alcohol** - Manufacturers and purveyors of alcohol.

> *Wine is a mocker and beer a brawler; whoever is led astray by them is not wise* (Proverbs 20:1).

But now I am writing you that you must not associate with anyone who calls himself a brother but is sexually immoral or greedy, an idolater or a slanderer, a drunkard or a swindler. With such a man do not even eat (1 Corinthians 5:11).

The long record of those who have been harmed by addiction to alcohol makes this area of investment hands-off for many Christians. This also is a classic example of why sin stocks appeal to other investors. Some investors appreciate the built-in market buried in the habits of addicts who cannot stop themselves from drinking. Add the subtle ways of advertising aimed at increasingly younger drinkers, and the market keeps growing even though the evils of this product are quite well known.

- **Gambling and gaming** - Casino and hotel operators who rely on gaming equipment, manufacturers who provide gaming items, Internet specialty companies who promote gaming online.

    For this reason God sends them a powerful delusion so that they will believe the lie and so that all will be condemned who have not believed the truth but have delighted in wickedness (2 Thessalonians 11-12).

> *A greedy man brings trouble to his family, but he who hates bribes will live* (Proverbs 15:27).

Some of you may identify with people who love to go to Las Vegas or to Atlantic City and look at it like the cost of any vacation. Others who enjoy gambling tell me they never lose, but if that were true, one would not see the incredible buildings and hotels in the gambling meccas. As the passage in Thessalonians reminds us, the palaces of the gambling casinos is a tribute to the losers, not those who claim to win all the time. The real sin here is the false impression that you can get rich quick or get something for nothing—one that often ensnares. Addiction in this arena is not uncommon either, although the families who suffer from the problem gambler are not as well known as those who suffer from alcohol, drug, and smoking addictions. Gambling promotes poverty since it appeals to those who can least afford to lose.

- **Corporate governance** - Companies who overpay their executives at the expense of their workers, companies who shower stock options on their management with no accountability, managements who will not consider the rights of shareholders, companies who slide huge compensation packages through the proxies with no financial information on the cost of such packages, managements who exclude major parts of the corporate team from decision making, Companies that forge mergers and restructurings for personal gain.

> *The integrity of the upright guides them, but the unfaithful are destroyed by their duplicity* (Proverbs 11:3-4).

> *Do not be misled: "Bad company corrupts good character." Come back to your senses as you ought, and stop sinning; for there are some who are ignorant of God—I say this to your shame* (1 Corinthians 15: 33-34).

There are too many examples of companies and their management that have turned money-grubbing when given opportunities to sell out, go do a leveraged buyout, backdate stock options or stack their compensation committee so that their paychecks look more like the GDP of a medium-sized country than that of a corporation.

- **Environmental negligence** - Companies that pollute the environment, companies that ignore the legal structure for preserving the environment, managements who make selfish short-term decisions that affect the environment.

> *For everything God created is good, and nothing is to be rejected if it is received with thanksgiv-*

*ing, because it is consecrated by the word of God prayer (*1 Timothy 4:4-5).

*The earth is the Lord's, and everything in it, the world, and all who live in it; for he founded it upon the seas and established it upon the waters. Who may ascend the hill of the Lord? Who may stand in his holy place? He who has clean hands and a pure heart, who does not lift up his soul to an idol or swear by what is false (*Psalm 24:1-4).

This is an issue that eludes many Christians for some reason, and it is unclear to me why so little has been done by the current group of BRI providers to address companies that violate the environment. Perhaps there is a delicate balance in evaluating companies in this realm because many very responsible companies work in industries that can be polluters. The oil industry comes to mind, and the work that many in this industry do to avoid problems is still not enough to avoid some incredibly ugly accidents.

For example, the spill of the Exxon Valdez tanker wreaked havoc on our environment, and yet, in the aftermath of that spill, ExxonMobil made great strides to show its positive side in the cleanup and in the prevention of future spills. Without responsible people in the companies that extract resources for the energy needs of our economy, the environment would be in even worse shape than it is.

BP has compounded the problem by their bungling attempts to balance their short term profit needs against the sound principles of safe extraction methods. Just the right amount of government regulation and oversight will encourage productivity while observing safety and conservation needs.

Shareholders can have influence in their company by insisting on being a better steward of God's creation! That being said, we could do better! The scare tactics in many of the arguments about global warming are still not to be overshadowed by the truth of many changes that are taking place in the way we use the world's resources. The disproportionate consumption of energy, where the U.S. uses up to 25 percent of the world's resources for less than 5 percent of the world's populace, is not a great legacy. Investors also would do well to take note of how their companies are dealing with the environment in their businesses. Conservation and pollution concerns ought to be a believer's concern as we adopt the same responsibilities for stewardship of our Creation as we do for other resources.

■ ■ ■ ■ ■

The above list of issues identifies the major concerns of most Biblically Responsible Investors. This does not mean you must have interest in every single one in order to become a responsible investor. However, if you choose to use an investor who subscribes to this process, these are the most likely issues that will be considered.

Biblically Responsible Investing is a tool to help us fulfill our responsibility to God and to others. An important guide for Christians can be found in Romans 13 and 14. I encourage you to read these two chapters. They are filled with valuable guidance for life. An entire book could be (and obviously has been) written on these words, but I want to make two simple observations that apply to Christian stewardship.

Every person is to be in subjection to the governing authorities. For there is no authority except from God, and those which exist are established by God. Therefore whoever resists authority has opposed the ordinance of God; and they who have opposed will receive condemnation upon themselves. For rulers are not a cause of fear for good behavior, but for evil. Do you want to have no fear of authority? Do what is good and you will have praise from the same; for it is a minister of God to you for good. But if you do what is evil, be afraid; for it does not bear the sword for nothing; for it is a minister of God, an avenger who brings wrath on the one who practices evil. Therefore it is necessary to be in subjection, not only because of wrath, but also for conscience' sake. For because of this you also pay taxes, for rulers are servants of

God, devoting themselves to this very thing. Render to all what is due them: tax to whom tax is due; custom to whom custom; fear to whom fear; honor to whom honor.

Owe nothing to anyone except to love one another; for he who loves his neighbor has fulfilled the law. For this, "You shall not commit adultery, You shall not murder, You shall not steal, You shall not covet," and if there is any other commandment, it is summed up in this saying, "You shall love your neighbor as yourself." Love does no wrong to a neighbor; therefore love is the fulfillment of the law.

Do this, knowing the time, that it is already the hour for you to awaken from sleep; for now salvation is nearer to us than when we believed. The night is almost gone, and the day is near. Therefore let us lay aside the deeds of darkness and put on the armor of light. Let us behave properly as in the day, not in carousing and drunkenness, not in sexual promiscuity and sensuality, not in strife and jealousy. But put on the Lord Jesus Christ, and make no provision for the flesh in regard to its lusts.

Now accept the one who is weak in faith, but not for the purpose of passing judgment on his opinions. One person has faith that he may eat all things, but he who is weak eats vegetables only. The one who eats is not to regard with contempt the one who does not eat, and the one who does not eat is not to judge the one who eats, for God has accepted him. Who are you to judge the servant of another? To his own master he stands or falls; and he will stand, for the Lord is able to make him stand.

One person regards one day above another, another regards every day alike. Each person must be fully convinced in his own mind. He who observes the day, observes it for the Lord, and he who eats, does so for the Lord, for he gives thanks to God; and he who eats not, for the Lord he does not eat, and gives thanks to God. For not one of us lives for himself, and not one dies for himself; for if we live, we live for the Lord, or if we die, we die for the Lord; therefore whether we live or die, we are the Lord's. For to this end Christ died and lived again, that He might be Lord both of the dead and of the living.

But you, why do you judge your brother? Or you again, why do you regard your brother with contempt? For we will all stand before the judgment seat of God. For it is written, "As I live, says the Lord, every knee shall bow to Me, And every tongue shall give praise to God." So then each one of us will give an account of himself to God.

Therefore let us not judge one another anymore, but rather determine this—not to put an obstacle or a stumbling block in a brother's way. I know and am convinced in the Lord Jesus that *nothing is unclean in itself; but to him who thinks anything to be unclean, to him it is unclean. For if because of food your brother is hurt, you are no longer walking according to love. Do not destroy with your food him for whom Christ died. Therefore do not let what is for you a good thing be spoken of as evil; for the kingdom of God is not eating and drinking, but righteousness and peace and joy in the Holy Spirit. For he who in this way serves Christ is acceptable to God and approved by men. So then we pursue the things which make for peace and the building up of one another. Do not tear down the work of God for the sake of food. All things indeed are clean, but they are evil for the man who eats and gives offense. It is good not to eat meat or to drink wine, or to do anything by which your brother stumbles. The faith which you have, have as your own conviction before God. Happy is he who does not condemn himself in what he approves. But he who doubts is condemned if he eats, because his eating is not from faith; and whatever is not from faith is sin.* (Romans 13-14)

The first truth is that we live in community and it is important to be good citizens of that community. These verses remind us over and over that we live in relationship with one another. The Apostle Paul begins with the reminder that we have authorities placed over us for our benefit. We are not to live in fear of these authorities but in subjection to them since God uses them for our benefit. This was a powerful statement given the context of Paul's writing. The rule of Rome was not an easy life for first-century Christians.

From an explanation of our responsibility to be good citizens, Paul makes a very smooth segue into the truth that we have a duty to one another—to love. Using references to several of the Ten Commandments, he explains what it means practically to love our neighbor. The best resource we have for accomplishing this task is to live a pure life. We must always be conscious that we are living for Christ. With that foundation, we will certainly be good citizens and good neighbors.

The point I want us to see in this concept is our responsibility to one another. When it comes to making stewardship decisions we must make them with the knowledge that we do not live in a vacuum. What we do with our money makes a direct impact on others. This is such a simple concept that we tend to forget. The store I choose to shop for groceries will benefit from my expenditure. They can hire more people who will then benefit from the food I choose to eat.

For many years, this idea of living in a community caused us to place a great deal of emphasis on shopping locally. In other words, we wanted to purchase as much as possible from neighborhood merchants in order to support our local community.

Times have changed. We now live in a global community. It is common to speak with people on the opposite side of the world, to watch real time video from anywhere, and to receive ordered goods within twenty-four hours. In fact, Amazon is currently working on plans to implement same day delivery when we order online. What this means is that we can impact people who are very far away from us with the way we use our money and resources. In other words, our community is very large.

Living in community still includes the way we relate to our next door neighbors and those who attend our church. However, it also extends to the footprint we leave around the world with every transaction we make. Although this might sound like forboding information, it is actually a very good situation. It means we have the ability to make a positive impact in far greater ways than ever imagined.

Not only can I spend my money in a way that helps my local grocer, but I can also spend it in a way that helps a poor family in India. The size of our community is staggering and as Christians, we have a responsibility to work and strive for the best for that community and one another. The way we invest our money plays a valuable role in helping us accomplish this task. Expressing it as simply as possible, we can invest in a company that creates jobs in third-world countries or in a company that is causing environmental damage. To be a good citizen of our community requires more than sending our money to a financial planner with the charge to make as much profit as possible.

The second truth of Romans 13 and 14 is the importance of living out our convictions. At the conclusion of the fourteenth chapter, Paul instructs us to be faithful to our convictions. When it comes to money and finances, this is an area where Christians have often been lacking. We speak of Jesus being Lord of our lives but one of the last areas of our life that we turn over to Him to control is our money.

There is a legend (perhaps with a kernel of truth) about Sam Houston, an early leader and politician in Texas. The story goes that Houston was being baptized and as he waded into the creek it was suggested that he leave his wallet on dry ground. Houston declined, saying that he wanted to be baptized completely, money and all.

There are no clauses in the life of a disciple that allow us to withhold certain areas of life from Jesus. Our living is to be consistent with our conviction. If we are convinced that Jesus is Lord, then He is to have influence over all decisions, including spending and investing decisions. This has practical implications that are addressed by Biblically Responsible Investing. For example, if you are convinced that abortion is wrong, in order to live consistently with that conviction, it would be irresponsible to make any investments that promote, encourage, or facilitate abortions.

Biblically Responsible Investing provides a tool for living consistently with our convictions. Not only do we take a stand with our words that we oppose certain behaviors and support other actions, but we can also take a stand with our money. It is not beyond reason to think that if enough Christians took this approach, it would be possible to make some significant changes in the way many companies operate. It is true that money speaks very loudly.

What Can I Expect from Biblically Responsible Investing

One of the first concerns you might have about Biblically Responsible Investing, and one voiced by many who consider the subject, is what you can expect financially if you choose to adopt this type of investing. It is certainly a reasonable question since the main reason people invest is in order to realize a profit. However, before I say anything about the financial implications, I want to point out the most important result of this type of investing–the spiritual benefit to you and others.

You will no longer need to be concerned that your investments are funding sinful activities. Like the two faithful servants in Jesus' parable we discussed earlier, you can anticipate the Master's words, "Well done, good and faithful servant." This is a tremendous benefit, which should be sufficient by itself, even without financial considerations.

However, you are making investments, so naturally you are concerned about the rate of return. It is natural to ask if you must sacrifice financially in order to have your investments screened according to Biblically Responsible Investments guidelines. There are three possible outcomes when you consider investment performance. If you shift all of your investments to follow BRI patterns one of three things will happen: First, it is possible you will attain superior performance. Second, you might match the same performance as if you were in a secular portfolio. Finally, you might receive a lower return than if you were in a secular portfolio. Because most of you will not have a problem with the first or second, let's assume most of your concern will be in dealing with the third event.

Suppose you felt God's calling in this, and it was obvious that the investments you were holding were indeed more in line with your Christian worldview, but those companies were not doing well. If the indexes were performing at 10 percent and you were earning eight or nine percent, would you still believe that it would be more important to go back to owning companies that would be offensive to God? Every investment strategy other than indexing will have this variance from the norm during some stretch of their investment history. Even when you are doing God's will, the performance of your investments will not always carry a superior return.

The fact is, BRI providers are competing in the secular marketplace. While there is a need to show investors that there may be a cost to being a BRI investor, my belief is that investors who invest this way will profit both short and long term. But it is really about being honest with all concerned to show credible comparisons.

Performance statistics is one of the most abused and slanted areas of the financial services industry. The most strongly stated case I can give you from my experience on Wall Street is that BRI providers as a whole, will, over time, perform in a similar fashion to their secular competitors. If this is not enough to put you at ease about performance, then you are free to keep chasing rainbows and looking for the pot of gold. If anything, watch out for the incredible "out performers" as they may be overstating their numbers or even worse be padding their numbers similar to other "Ponzi" schemers. At the very least, they are probably guilty of using the wrong benchmark to overstate their performance which I would call a sin of commission!

It is impossible, and foolish, to make promises about investments, but experience shows you are not likely to do any worse financially with BRI. However, you have the added benefit of making investments that are consistent with your spiritual beliefs. There is really no way to put a value on that experience. Businesses that operate according to principles that benefit people are not necessarily less profitable. The reason God gave principles of stewardship in the first place is for our benefit. It is important to understand something about biblical principles. They are not rules or laws.

Rather, there are statements about how things work. Basically, a principles says, "If you do this, you can expect this result."

When we arrange our lives according to God's principles we can expect blessing. This is very true in the financial realm. If we choose to spend and invest our money according to God's desires, we should not worry about loss or missed opportunities. Instead we can expect to experience the blessings of God. This is why BRI is such a powerful tool for investors.

Another important consideration is the power you can wield as a shareholder in a company. It is incorrect to think that the only course of action for a Biblically Responsible Investor is to sell off all unacceptable stocks. To do so is to neglect an important tool you can use for good.

First Data Corp (FDC) was the centerpiece of a controversy a few years back when it was being screened out by money managers who were trying to avoid companies that were not living up to the standards set by many believers. The point of contention stemmed around the fact that this company had a great track record and growth trend that was developed from processing credit cards. One of the fastest-growing segments of FDC's business was in the area of pornography. As the awareness of this was growing, one broker discovered that his firm had just placed a buy recommendation on FDC. The broker called the analyst and asked why the analyst would recommend a company that had such a large exposure to porn. The analyst confessed he was not aware of the extent of the exposure to the pornography industry. The rather confused analyst reworked his numbers, and one month later pulled the recommendation. A little more than a year later, FDC decided to get out of the business of dealing with the porn industry, and the company then became a favorite of several of the same BRI money managers who just one year earlier were thumbs down on it. This is not an effort to connect the dots and indicate that FDC changed their corporate strategy because of one pulled analyst rating—but who knows?

Should you make the radical move of immediately selling all inappropriate assets and withdraw completely from investing? (How does one do that in today's world anyway?) Or should you simply ignore your newfound knowledge and look the other way? It is common for some well-meaning Christians to take a defensive position over their investments because the offending companies also may be lauded as leaders of American industry. They participate in our dynamic economy with growth and productivity, and they have provided paychecks and comfortable retirement plans for many people. That doesn't excuse them, however, if they are sponsoring activities that oppose Christianity.

The sad fact is, the likelihood that you own one or more of these stocks is quite high unless you already have done your homework and researched these companies to discover what they are doing in all areas of their corporate outreach. Even if you don't own these stocks individually, if you invest in mutual funds it is still very likely that your fund will own many of these companies. As a shareholder, you are a fractional owner in that company.

As a Christian shareholder, you have an additional responsibility to act as God's proxy. Consider this: By always giving approval for any proposal of management, you have helped endorse the actions of that company. Voting with management without thinking about the consequences has been a longstanding tradition that the managements of public corporations take into consideration and rely upon. By throwing your proxy in the wastebasket or automatically marking it with management, you may have been unwittingly complicit to sinful activities conducted by corporate America. As long as you hold part ownership in a company, you have some say as to how it is run.

It is time to start reading the annual reports of the companies in your portfolio if you are making the investment decisions. Then, after reading the annual reports, it is important to complete and vote the proxy forms for each company. Many will scoff at this as it is difficult to think that one vote will make a difference in the world of corporate governance as it exists today. Never forget that one vote here and one vote there could add up to a lot of changes in the way public companies are being run. Stop throwing the proxy in the wastebasket on top of the annual report! Do you realize every time you do, the people who run these companies are free to exercise their will without getting input from the owners...that's you by the way! In case you haven't realized it, those presidents and chairmen of the boards are supposed to work for you!

Take a big-picture view of each company in the portfolio. What is the business of the company? Do you believe that any of their activities would fall into the list of inappropriate investments that Christian money managers weed out when building their portfolios? Do any of the companies in your portfolio, in fact, show an effort to be part of the solution we seek as Christian investors, by conducting themselves in an exemplary way in dealing with the public?

You may want to write to the company directly and ask if any of its operations are violating your concerns as a Christian. You also might purchase research on this subject. It is just as important, however, to look at what companies are doing right and not to be obsessed with the sins of companies. Too often Christians are seen as only emphasizing the negative, and in many cases this is a legitimate criticism.

Jesus used two metaphors that clearly speak to the issue of Biblically Responsible Investing.

You are the salt of the earth; but if the salt has become tasteless, how can it be made salty again? It is no longer good for anything, except to be thrown out and trampled under foot by men.

You are the light of the world. A city set on a hill cannot be hidden; nor does anyone light a lamp and put it under a basket, but on the lampstand, and it gives light to all who are in the house. Let your light shine before men in such a way that they may see your good works, and glorify your Father who is in heaven (Matthew 5:13-16).

The first metaphor is that Jesus calls us the salt of the earth. Salt is a very powerful thing, packing a punch far beyond its size and appearance. If you are not convinced of the power of salt to make a difference, try adopting a "salt-free" diet. You will need to adjust to the taste of bland food. In order for salt to have any value it must first permeate. It preserves meat by dissolving into the meat; it melts ice by dissolving in the ice. Salt has no value when it is in the saltshaker. We are the ones who flavor and preserve the world. Without followers of Christ, the world becomes a tasteless, putrid place.

It is a problem when we are tempted to believe that we have fulfilled our role as salt when we show up at church on occasion. We might even feel especially "salty" if we invite a friend to come visit our saltshaker for a special Christmas show. It has become easy to define being a disciple of Jesus to mean little more than attending church. The truth is that we have to get out into the world to make a difference.

As a Christian investor, you have the opportunity to bring salt, with its flavoring and preserving qualities, into the marketplace. To be a faithful steward requires rolling up your sleeves and doing some diligent work in order to make a difference.

Jesus' second metaphor is light—we are the light of the world. It is our task to provide light so others can find their way. Just like salt cannot be contained, neither should light be hidden. As an investor you have an opportunity to use your investments to shine the light on companies and their behavior. It can be a tool to lead them to more appropriate activities and behavior.

As we have noted repeatedly, a good steward does more than simply turn their money over for others to use and return a profit. Those who will be known as "good and faithful" will be those who are involved with how the money is used and what it is accomplishing.

How Do I Get Started With Biblically Responsible Investing

The place to start is to find a Christian financial investor you can trust. What do Christian financial advisors bring to the marketplace? If you are an investor, here is a list of questions to ask to help you identify a financial advisor who is interested in bringing Christianity into his practice:

- Does your advisor ever ask you about your faith journey to see if it is important in how you are investing your funds?

- Is there clear communication in regard to how your advisor charges for their services? (Commissions, fees, expenses for services, etc.)

- Has your advisor indicated any experience in screening investment choices to reflect a Christian worldview?

- Would your advisor pray with you and ask God's blessings on you?

- Do you feel confident that your advisor is looking at you instead of your money?

- Would you trust this advisor to help your children, grandchildren, or a sick relative?

- Is this advisor knowledgeable in a wide variety of subjects, especially in finance?

If you are a mutual fund investor, it is time to start searching for a mutual fund that invests like your heart and your Bible teaches you. Read the prospectus of the funds before you invest and decide if this way of investing sounds pleasing to God and to you. Keep looking and searching to find the fund or funds that you are comfortable with. Always look at the top five or ten holdings in a fund; they also will give you a clue as to the type of companies in which the firm is placing its strongest weightings.

If you invest on your own in individual stocks and bonds, find out as much as you can about the companies before buying or retaining them. Ask your advisor about how to best screen for companies that you, as a Christian, wish to avoid. Once you have built a portfolio, there are some benefits from direct ownership in stocks. In addition to receiving the annual reports directly from the companies you own, you also will receive a proxy to vote as you wish, regarding corporate matters. All of these are available online, as well as through snail mail. When the proxy comes each year, vote it! Don't throw it away! When you see most proxies, you will find they are very minimal on information and very strong on advocating how to vote. It is often true that agreeing with management helps the shareholders.

What can investors and advisors do? They can make choices from several providers of BRI services and work with their advisors to start screening for biblical purposes, starting with money managers who don't really want to do it. No matter the inclinations of others, it is God's money you are entrusted with, and if a money manager is unwilling to help you screen unwanted holdings, find a new manager! Currently, only about 1% of all investments are screened using BRI principles. Investors must demand choices that include BRI-screened alternatives if the industry is to reach critical mass and become a credible alternative. Until that time when there are greater resources to help, each investor is urged to spend time checking out the work being done by a handful of providers.

■ ■ ■ ■ ■

By this point, it already should be obvious that most of us have fallen short in our duties and responsibilities as they relate to being responsible Christian shareholders. By conceding the moral ground to others who neither read nor care about biblical truth, we have allowed a secular society to force moral principles upon us that brought sexual sin, materialism, and impurity of all types to a level of acceptance that now require us to recover this "stolen" property.

Given the history of many movements that get started with good intentions, Christians have often seen how good intentions can turn into bad results. For example, when many jumped on the bandwagon about the pitfalls of our society moving into the 21st century, we had snake oil salesmen spouting Scripture and inciting a Y2K panic. Likewise, many of our country's financial hardships are compounded by some taking advantage of the poor. Debt, including the government's deficits, is cited as cause and effect for more maladies than I can imagine. Because almost everyone has a mortgage or some debt on credit cards, whole industries have been developed to deal with that guilt trip. Our best hope for success in the BRI movement is that believers start to take stewardship seriously, not only in their portfolios, but also as it relates to their relationship with God.

A New Story Continued

The day scheduled for Todd's meeting with his investors and friends came quicker than he would have liked. It always seems the case when you want to give something your best that you have a nagging feeling you should have done more preparation. He and Elise spent many mornings dissecting the subject as they shared their morning coffee on the backyard deck. The warm summer mornings made it comfortable for them to spend extended periods of time enjoying the outdoors.

Knowing that he needed more guidance than what he and Elise could devise, Todd turned to the Internet to see if he could find more information. Sloshing through a variety of Google searches, he came upon something called, "Biblically Responsible Investing."

As he read about this investment tool he quickly realized this was not a new thing—Christians have been utilizing this method for handing their finances for a long time. It was good to know he could find help once he and Elise embarked on this journey.

The investor meeting was scheduled for early Tuesday morning. There was really nothing formal about the planned gathering. All of these guys had shared many hours together over the years, normally over a meal or reminiscing about old times. Todd was prepared to share his concerns but he was not planning to make any type of formal presentation—he just wanted to share his heart.

Brett had already briefed everyone concerning the purpose of the meeting so after they shared a few pleasantries, grabbed a cup of coffee, and sat down in the small conference room, Todd knew it was time to begin. The first thing he did, which made him slightly uncomfortable because he had never done this before with this group, was to ask if he could lead a prayer. Todd ignored a couple of wise cracks from his friends as he lowered his head and began to pray and ask for God's guidance.

It took ten or fifteen minutes for Todd to recount his journey, beginning with meeting Robert Wells at church and his request concerning his ownership in the building that housed the abortion clinic. Not all of the investors were aware their property was being used for performing abortions before Todd brought it to their attention a week earlier.

As Todd was speaking, Nelson Smith, the one who had always been known as the life of the party during their younger days, spoke up and asked, "So, what are we supposed to do?"

The others were a little taken aback because it was unusual for Nelson to ever say anything serious. However, no one was surprised when Bill Williams blurted out, "We should just throw them out!" It was typical of Bill of do something first and then think about it second.

As the one operating the business, Brett knew he would be the one on the front lines so he cautioned, "Let's think about this first. We need to decide if we want to lose one of our best tenants or not."

Almost in union, several voices inquired, "When is their lease up?"

Everyone expected meticulous preparation from Brett so all eyes focused on him as he opened a folder with the name "Uptown Women's Clinic" typed on the protruding tab. "The lease is up at the end of the year, about six more months," he explained.

"Is there any way we can get out of it?" asked Nelson.

"I've read through it several times… the've been good tenants, always getting the rent on time… never any problem. I don't see any legal cause for terminating the lease."

Discussion continued for several minutes and

it was clearly the consensus something needed to be done but there was little to do until the lease expired. At that time they could seek a new tenant.

Todd was pleased his friends understood and agreed with his concern. He was a little apprehensive about going home and reporting to Elise that nothing could be done for several months. She had little patience for waiting when she felt something needed to happen. He thought it was worth putting something else on the table. "How about a couple of us speak with the clinic to express our concerns. It probably won't make much difference, but it wouldn't hurt to talk. Maybe if they knew we were not going to renew the lease unless they made some changes... I don't know. I think it's worth a try."

As you might imagine, Todd and Brett were assigned the task. Todd left the meeting hopeful that something could be done. In his experience it is always a good sign when two sides can agree to discuss an issue.

He felt good driving home. He was beginning to feel more like a good steward, the kind described in Jesus' parable. He also had a meeting scheduled for later in the week with his financial planner. He and Elise were going to speak with him about instituting the BRI screens to their portfolio. This whole thing might turn into more work than he first thought, but if he could use the resources God put in his hands in a way to benefit others, it would be well worth it.

■ ■ ■ ■ ■

Todd's hope was that Elise would join him on the visit to their financial planner to discuss changing the focus of their investments. However, Sarah and Christopher were back from their honeymoon and Sarah wanted to spend the day shopping with her mom. Apparently exchanging wedding gifts and spending the day with her daughter were more important than their investments. It wasn't surprising since Todd took care of the majority of financial business for the family.

Wallace Burke had all the trappings of success. His professionally styled office suite was located on the third floor of the Overton Bank Building in the heart of the city. The polished tile floor in the hallway led to an oversized mahogany door with silver-plated hardware. Once you stepped inside, the carpet was plush, the furniture was rich, and the colors were subdued. Margaret, a woman appearing to be in her 50's and always dressed as conservatively as a grandmother, had been Wallace's secretary for years and her voice was the first thing heard when entering the office suite.

"Hello Mr. Watson," was her cheery greeting. She did not need to have Wallace's calendar in front of her to recognize Todd. He had been investing according to Wallace's financial advice for years and was probably his best customer. There was no need to sit, Wallace was ready and waiting in his office, so Margaret quickly escorted Todd as if he were a new customer.

Not being sure why Todd wanted the meeting, Wallace had all his paperwork in order, spread out on top of his executive-style desk. He and Todd liked each other, but they had never spent any time together outside of their business relationship. Wallace was several years older and pretty tied to a quiet routine. No one would ever say that Wallace liked adventure or taking risks and he ran his investments like he ran his life–as risk free as possible.

Todd and Wallace exchanged the usual pleasantries. Margaret brought Todd a cup of coffee, just like he liked it, and they sat down to discuss the matter that brought Todd unexpectedly to the office.

"I know you're curious about why I'm here," Todd began. "First, let me assure you that it is not because I'm unhappy with anything you've done! Elise and I have been very pleased with the way you have handled the money. You have accomplished precisely what we asked you to do for us."

The words provided a touch of assurance for Wallace but he was still waiting for something more. He knew Todd was not there just to pat him on the back. "We want you to continue managing our money," Todd said, and Wallace hoped his sigh of relief was not visible. "It's just that we want to change our approach," Todd continued.

"Your investments have been doing very well," Wallace replied, "Especially in this economy. I'm not sure we can do much better." He was hoping Todd was not looking for a bigger payday that required riskier investments, that was just not Wallace's strength.

"No, no, I'm not concerned about making more money. Elise and I have been thinking a lot lately about how our money is being used. Let me explain how this whole thing came up."

Todd then took the next seven or eight minutes to describe the encounter with Robert Wells at church and how that turned into the conversation with his business partners and then the questions they had about all their money and what it was accomplishing. He also tried to explain how he had spent hours reflecting on Jesus' story of the talents and his conviction that God was trying to tell him something about being a better steward. Wallace listened carefully. He was certainly interested in Todd's way of thinking because good investment advisors must know their clients and he always prided himself on being able to provide what his clients wanted.

When Todd brought up the phrase, "Biblically Responsible Investing" that he had read about on the Internet, Wallace's attitude changed. He was somewhat defensive toward this approach to investing. Making money in this volatile market was not an easy thing to do and Todd should be happy that Wallace is getting him a decent return. Now he wants to put some stipulations on how to invest and will probably be upset if he doesn't make as much money.

"What do you know about investing like this?" Todd asked.

"I've studied it some, "replied Wallace hesitantly. "I'm not convinced it's a good way to go."

Somewhat surprised since he knew Wallace was a Christian, Todd pressed, "Tell me why, I'd like to know."

"Probably my first concern is the financial loss you will experience, or at least the financial opportunity missed, by not investing in some very profitable companies, just because we don't agree with everything they do." This was always Wallace's first comment when asked about BRI even though he didn't know of any evidence to prove it was true. It simply makes sense; if you avoid certain types of companies then you will likely miss some good opportunities.

Todd was expecting this objection since he had done his homework prior to the meeting. "Just because a company avoids questionable activities doesn't necessarily make it less profitable does it?" he asked.

"Not necessarily," agreed Wallace, "But if we change our investment habits just to avoid some of these issues, we might take a hit on your returns and that would not be good stewardship either." Keeping his investments separate from his religion seemed like a good policy to Wallace.

Sensing that Todd was not convinced, Wallace continued. "Besides, you know how difficult it is to determine exactly what companies are doing. A company that primarily makes dog food might have some secondary interests in tobacco or alcohol, or a computer company might hold ownership of a casino. I don't know if there is such a thing as a completely responsible company in today's world. Besides, I think this might just be a fad that will disappear in a short while. You know how investment fads come and go all the time."

"This is more than a fad with me, I really think this is something I want to consider. I know it's not easy," Todd said, trying to keep his aggravation toward Wallace's attitude from coming through his voice. "But it's important enough to me that I want to give it a try. What do we need to do to get started?"

"Like I've always said, I work for you," Wallace quickly chimed in once he realized Todd was committed to this new approach. "Give me a few days to get some information together and then we can meet and make some decisions."

"Great!" said Todd. "I'm ready as soon as we can get started."

They spoke a few more minutes, making plans to meet in exactly one week to formulate a plan. Todd was not totally pleased with the conversation but he was willing to give Wallace an opportunity. He had earned that much since he had been a good advisor for many years.

On the way out of the office, Todd spoke to Margaret, "I'll see you next week."

It was a short walk to the parking lot and just as he reached out with his left hand to open the car door, Todd's phone rang. As he had done countless times before without having to think, Todd reached into his pocket, pushed the answer button as he lifted the phone to his ear and said, "Hello."

"Todd, this is James," and then a very brief pause. "How are you doing?"

Without even looking at the caller id, Todd recognized the voice as James Adams, his pastor and good friend. He and James had been friends for more than six years, since James first came to the church as pastor. They were about the same age, both shared an interest in old cars, occasional fishing trips, and their wives were good friends. Put all that together with James' interest in Todd's spiritual growth and a close friendship developed.

Todd had already spoken with James about his interest in BRI. It came up in a conversation after discussing James' sermon on the parable of the talents. James knew a little about the subject. Obviously he did not have the money to invest like Todd, but he did keep a close eye on his retirement funds, which were managed by a Christian ministry that specialized in helping pastors.

"I'm good! Todd answered. "I'll bet with this weather you are wanting to plan a fishing trip."

"I would love to go fishing, but it's not gonna happen today. Hey, I called your office and they said you didn't have anything scheduled for lunch. I've got a proposition for you."

Both men enjoyed having lunch together but they were both too busy to make it happen often. "I'll tell you what, Todd responded, "name the place and I'll buy. How's that for a deal?"

"I knew you'd say that. Let me tell you what I have in mind. I'm having lunch with the man who handles my retirement account. After our conversation last week I thought you might want to meet him and pick his brain a little about responsible investing. What do you think?" asked James.

"That's a great idea James, perfect timing. Tell me when and where and I'll be there."

By the time the arrangements were shared Todd was in his car and driving out of the parking lot. He knew Elise and Sarah would be having lunch together so he was not worried about checking in. He had just enough time to make a couple of quick stops along the way to the restaurant.

The plan was to meet at Bronson's out on Westridge Parkway not far from the church. Although it was a new place it was rapidly becoming a favorite for James and several of their other friends from church. It was clean, the food was good, and the prices reasonable; all good reasons to chose a restaurant.

Traffic was light so Todd suspected he was a few minutes earlier than planned. He scanned the parking lot for James' car as he walked toward the entrance.

Confirming with the hostess that he was the first one there, he requested a table in the corner, hoping to be a quiet enough place to allow conversation. By the time the waiter took his order for a glass of water, Todd spotted James walking toward the table.

He stood up, grasped his hand firmly and said, "Hey friend, I'm so glad you called."

"I'm glad you could come," replied James. "Let me introduce my friend."

Pointing to a tall, slender man in a light tan sport coat, James said, "Todd, this is Michael McDonald, he is the financial advisor I told you about."

Todd and Michael shook hands and exchanged customary greetings. Todd said, "Thanks for including me in this conversation." Turning toward Michael he added, "James has probably told you about my interest in Biblically Responsible Investing."

"Yes, I was excited to hear about you. I've been trying to get the word out for several years but it has been difficult. Anytime I find a potential convert I'm like a preacher meeting a first time visitor at church."

All three men chuckled at the comment and the waiter arrived at the table at the same time to take drink orders and explain the menu. James and Todd knew what they wanted and Michael took their recommendation so there was no need to spend time studying the menu options. With the lunch order out of the way they could get about the business of discussion.

"What is the hardest thing about encouraging people into Biblically Responsible Investing?" posed Todd. "Why are Christians hesitant to take this approach?"

"I think the primary reason is that people don't like change. The ones who should be most interested in this type of investing are probably the same ones who strive to be good stewards. Consequently, they are reluctant to do anything that doesn't seem safe. They are making a little money by doing what everyone else is doing and most people equate that with being a good steward," answered Michael.

"That's exactly where I was until a few weeks ago," chimed in Todd. "Elise and I were happy that we were making some money, we were giving our tithe to the church and trying to manage our money carefully. Then I started reading Jesus' story of the talents. I don't know how many times I've read that story lately, but it won't let me go. We're convicted that we've got to do more."

About that time their lunch arrived. The waiter carefully arranged the table and made sure each of the men were satisfied. Talking stopped for a few minutes to allow everyone to sample the food and get started on the meal.

Todd was the first to get back on subject. "How hard is it to switch over to Biblically Responsible Investing?" he asked.

"It's not hard at all, not any more difficult than changing any investment in your portfolio," Michael responded. "All you need is a financial planner who is willing to help."

"That might be my problem," Todd said with a hint of dejection in his voice. "I just met with my guy this morning about making some changes and I'm not sure he's on board. I don't think he's opposed to the idea... just not confident in what to do."

Hoping to be reassuring, Michael said, "That's not uncommon. It's a new thing for a lot of financial planners. It's not that they are unwilling. They just need some help to get started."

"I think that's probably the problem," Todd replied. "He has always been very capable. What can I do to help?"

"I don't want to butt in, but maybe I can help. If you will give me permission, I'll call your guy and offer to help him get up to speed. There's no need for you to change planners if he's willing to make a little effort. In fact, it will make him a better planner for all his Christian investors."

This sounded like a good plan to Todd. He made arrangements to have Wallace call Michael and hopefully they could all three get together to get things started. Todd felt much better about his potential for being a good steward. This whole thing was turning into a lot more work than Todd expected at the beginning, but it would be well worth it to hear the words, "Well done, good and faithful servant."

Conclusion

Our new friend Todd has learned a great deal about stewardship in a very short time. With that new knowledge he has an opportunity to utilize the resources God's has placed in his hands in a way that will make him a more faithful steward. The opportunity also awaits you. How will you respond?

The third servant in Jesus' parable, the one who was unfaithful, failed because he did not act on the knowledge he possessed. He knew the gold was not his but belonged to the master. We are told that he was "entrusted" with the money. Also, he knew the master was going to return and he would be held accountable for his stewardship. His response was to do as little as possible. Consequently, he failed.

God has placed a certain amount of gold (money) in your hands. He has entrusted you with the stewardship of that money. It is also true that He will hold you accountable for that stewardship. Just as Todd discovered, it is not enough to be content with earning a little interest. God's concerns go much deeper. Neither is it adequate to leave the responsibility to others. The stewardship belongs to each of us.

However, stewardship is not something to be feared. Rather, it is an opportunity to be grasped. With the money at your disposal you have the opportunity to make a difference in the world and in the lives of other people.

Here are some steps you can take if you are serious about Biblically Responsible Investing:

- Do a scripture study of biblical stewardship, focusing specifically on the responsibilities we have to help others.

- Do a Goggle Search of "Biblically Responsible Investing" and read articles and websites to determine if this is something for you.

- Get a copy of my book, "Kingdom Gains: What Every Christian Should Know Before Investing." This book provides a basic understanding as well as more technical information you should know.

- Talk to your current advisor about Biblically Responsible Investing. If he/she is not interested, find another advisor, one who will work for you and understands your desires.

- Speak with friends and family members who have investments. Ask if they know anything about Biblically Responsible Investing. They might have resources to help or perhaps you can invite them to take the journey with you.

Like the two faithful servants in Jesus' parable, you can be in a position to hear the Master say, "Well done, good and faithful servant…"

CPSIA information can be obtained at www.ICGtesting.com
Printed in the USA
BVOW02s0537231013

334421BV00002B/2/P